The Tennis Curmudgeon Speaks ...

Insights from 40 years in the game

Dave Kocak

Untiliwin Press
Buffalo, New York

Published by Untiliwin Press, 63 Courier Blvd, Buffalo NY 14217

ISBN xxxxxxxxxx

Dedication

This book is dedicated to Linda, Judy, Cindy and Andrea and all the underpaid, underappreciated front desk people in all tennis clubs everywhere. No club runs smoothly without them. No one gets more undeserved grief, even though they are part of the solution without being any part of the problem. They certainly have made me look more organized and responsible than I am, and I thank them sincerely.

In case I never write another tennis book, I'd better take this opportunity to thank all my tennis students over the years. I am grateful that you trusted me to help you along in this sport. I hope I didn't disappoint. For those of you who supported me when I wasn't very good at this, I am especially grateful. I hope I have gotten better.

Table of Contents

Introduction

SHOCKED! Actually "SHOCKED" barely describes it. I was baffled and bewildered by the overwhelmingly positive response to my first book "Tennis for the Rest of Us." And no, the accolades weren't all from family members or creditors. Even the online reviews were glowing; surprisingly positive comments from perfect strangers as well as the positively gushing reviews from the four or five shills I had enlisted to give the book a bump.

I needed to write that book. It encapsulated my thirty five years of teaching tennis and offered information and perspective that I had not seen anywhere else. I had to write it. It is my legacy.

This book I wrote for the money. Not really, there's not that much money to be had. I was tired of throwing things at the TV or the window of the tennis club or the table behind me at the tennis club when I heard or saw the stupidest things passing for wisdom and convention. I thought I would like to set the record straight or challenge the prevailing wisdom or share some insight gathered from forty years in the sport. It is meant to amuse, inform and stimulate your brain to see things from a different perspective, admittedly one that is twisted and skewed beyond all ordinary recognition.

With my humble background it takes a certain amount of ego to flaunt the system, and apparently I have more than enough for the task.

The views in this book are strictly my own (who else would claim them), but if you'd like to appropriate them, be my guest. Just know that you will be subject to the same amount of ridicule I receive, or perhaps more because everyone already knows I'm perverse.

This book covers three topics: playing the game, teaching the game, and the Pro game. Some of them overlap. Each and every topic stands alone and can be read out of order. "Observations" are mini-topics with no particular attachment to anything else in the book. Each can be read start to finish in one session in your own personal library.

I hope you enjoy it.

P.S. As a kid I loved reading Sherlock Holmes and I particularly liked how the titles of the stories almost never revealed anything, but always piqued your curiosity. Titles such as "The Blue Carbuncle", "The Sign of the Four" and "The Red Headed League" always made me want to wade in and find out what the hell Arthur Conan Doyle had on his mind. I've tried to do a little of that myself.

CHAPTER ONE

The Plan

Everyone needs a game plan. There is the general plan; this is how I like to play. Then there is the specific game plan; this is how I will adapt how I like to play to this particular opponent. The specific plan may be based on previous experience or may be the result of information from the warmup or might be made up as you go along. You start with what you like to do and adapt as the results dictate.

But here's the thing about plans. Sometimes they don't work. Sometimes they don't work because we don't execute them very well, sometimes they don't work because they weren't very good plans to begin with, and sometimes they don't work because *"We don't stick to the plan!"*

It's important to differentiate between bad plans and plans poorly executed. For instance, if your plan is to lob your opponent when he comes to the net and all your lobs are long, is this a bad plan or poorly executed? It could be you are not a good lobber or that his approaches are too good for you to hit a good lob, which makes this a poor plan. On the other hand, if this is just a bad lobbing day it may get better further into the match or you lose, but that doesn't make it a bad plan. If you are a 3.0 player and you decide to win with your one-handed backhand topspin lob, well...need I say anything more?

Here are a few illustrations of these points.

Peter B. was a fellow teaching pro working at the same resort as I was. Every week, along with the pros from the nearby camp, we had a tournament. The final tournament of the season had a little prize

9

money and I wound up against Peter B. in the final. Peter was an excellent player and definitely the favorite going into our match, but not an overwhelming favorite. He was long and lean and he choked up on the racquet about an inch. This seemed to give him excellent control, but not a lot of power. He had excellent groundstrokes and passing shots, great return of serve and a mediocre serve. He didn't come to the net a lot, but that wasn't significant because I planned to be there as much as possible.

Peter was the kind of guy that would look right at home in a Harvard professor's private library holding court with a bunch of students wearing a tweed coat with elbow patches and smoking a pipe. I'd never seen him rattled, on court or off.

The strength of my game was to serve and volley with a lefty slice serve to the backhand, particularly on the ad court and to come in whenever possible on his serve. Peter had a great backhand return, and since he had long arms, I thought the play would be to serve right at his body, and that's what I did.

Every time I was on the baseline thinking about where to serve, out wide to the backhand or forehand or straight at him, I chose straight at him. With the possible exception of a few serves at 40-love, I believe I hit 100% of my first serves into the body. And it worked. I got broken in the second set and lost that but was unbroken otherwise and won in three close sets.

Afterwards, after he had picked the fuzz out of his ribs, we both agreed that that strategy won me the match. It took a lot of discipline not to use a variety of serves, but it paid off. I am often not so disciplined.

Next illustration.

Bill P. was a big guy with a very good serve, good forehand and suspect backhand and definitely a better player than me. The court we were playing on was very fast making breaking his big serve a real problem. I was never a great service returner. On the bright side was that the fast court made my serve difficult for him. As long as I could serve and volley and force him to pass me with his shaky backhand, I had a shot.

Once again discipline might be the key. For six service games, I served, came in, volleyed to his backhand, and for six games he couldn't pass me often enough to break me. Unfortunately, I didn't break him either. Off to the tiebreaker we went. After five points on serve I served, came in and volleyed to his (are you freakin' kidding me) *forehand* where he easily passed me. That's all it took for the first set. I hadn't volleyed to his forehand for an hour and in a key moment in the tiebreaker I got cute. How does that happen? I think it had something to do with my Mother not loving me enough.

In the second set, I was even smarter. I think it was my third service game that I decided to volley to the forehand. I missed one (I'd only tried one in the last hour), he passed me on the second one and that was all it took. 7-6, 6-3. I told you discipline was the key. I didn't say I had it, just that it was the key.

Next illustration.

I was playing a good serve and volleyer whom I couldn't pass or lob often enough to get a break. Fortunately he was not doing any better. The weather was overcast and muggy and the balls were heavy. This wasn't Wimbledon with balls being changed every 7 or 9 games. Finally, I decided if I couldn't beat him staying on the baseline, I had to beat him at the net. I started coming in on everything; my serve, his serve and every other chance I got. It almost looked like a doubles match with everyone rushing the net. I looked awfully silly on a lot of those points, but I won a lot of them too. Eventually I won enough to win. As it turns out, I made the right adjustment.

Last illustration.

I watched my baseline friend play an aggressive serve and volleyer. In the first set my friend passed him consistently and won the first set handily. In the second, his opponent really crowded the net and those angled passing shots got cut off with what looked like some pretty spectacular volleys. The second set got away, and then the third, without one attempt to hit the ball over his head.

When I mentioned to my friend that his opponent had made an adjustment that he hadn't reacted to, I moved away quickly to avoid thrown objects. Just for the record, there is a good time and place to mention these things, but it's not right after the match.

I am not suggesting a good plan will help you when you are clearly overmatched, but it sure helps when you aren't.

One last quick story. My usual strategy is to attack the backhand and come to the net. Against this particular unknown opponent, I got passed with two very good looking two-handed backhands. I spent the next three hours trying to break down his forehand. I later learned that he had just switched to a two-handed backhand and those first two passing shots were the best ones of his life. If I had stayed with my normal strategy for a few more points I might have won easily.

I guess the lesson is not to give up on a plan too soon.

CHAPTER TWO

Mental Energy

Mental energy, for our purposes, is the ability to focus and concentrate to produce this moment's best possible tennis. What I mean by "this moment" is, under these circumstances, how good can I be? It might be 90 degrees in the shade with 90% humidity. Under these conditions you hope to survive. It's early in the first set on a perfectly gorgeous day. Under these conditions you hope to thrive.

Mental energy is finite. You only have so much of it for the match, and only so much for a tournament, assuming the matches are spaced relatively close together.

Daniel Kahneman in his great book "Thinking, fast and slow" describes two types of mental energy: Brain 1 and Brain 2 (he's obviously not one of those guys who brainstorms names like Cialis and Boniva and Allegra-D). Brain 1 is your conscious, problem solving brain and Brain 2 is your automatic pilot for more simple tasks. Have you ever found yourself driving home thinking about some problem and pulled into your driveway not remembering how you got there? That's Brain 1 problem solving as Brain 2 is driving. Brain 2 is cruise control, Brain 1 is WORK. Work is hard. It tires us out. Ask the air traffic controller on his way home from work looking forward to rolling around on the floor with his kids, but arrives to find that Jason and Alyssa both need help with their homework. Not a lot left in the tank for that activity.

Like I said, Mental energy is finite, to waste it is dangerous.

Where to begin?

Let's start with pre-match preparation.

Let's assume a weekday evening match. You're not playing until 6 o'clock but that doesn't mean you don't have to think about it all day. Prepare yourself mentally to play good tennis. Even though I have other things to do all day, that match is in the back of my mind all day. Once in a while it creeps to the front and I think about things like how to play this opponent or how successful I've been lobbing lately and to make sure I don't forget to do that.

Sure, you want to make sure you eat at the right time and the right food and make sure you are hydrated, especially in the heat, but you want to make sure you are in the right frame of mind as well.

On to the match.

Point number one: Our goal is to win the match, not a point or a game or a set. Of course you can't win the match without winning those other things, but our goal is to win the match and we do not need to celebrate any of those lesser victories.

A perfect illustration of this occurred while I was watching a good junior play a good older (30s) player from out of town in a tournament with a $500 first prize. A very competitive first set ended with the kid winning in a tiebreaker 13-11. He came off the court to get some water, all smiles as if he had just won. The veteran remained seated and when play resumed proceeded to show the kid exactly what he had won. The next two sets went by quickly as the old man won 6-1, 6-2. From the beginning of the first set until the last point of the match, there was no change in his demeanor. He knew when he lost the tiebreaker that he hadn't lost anything yet, nor had the kid won anything.

Point number two: It's more important to know how to win than to be ahead in the score. We enter many competitive matches with no idea of how to beat the other player or team. We know our strengths and weaknesses but don't much about them. Every game reveals a little more about them to us, and us to them. Whether we are winning or losing, we should be learning something along the way. Sometimes we just muddle through a match, not sure about much of anything. It's just as likely a win or a loss. But sometimes, hopefully oftentimes, your brain carves out what you believe is a winning strategy. Maybe she gets scared when you come to the net, or has a weak overhead when she comes to the net or has a backhand you are confident will break down if you keep hitting it there. Whatever it is, you are confident it will work. Does being ahead or behind at this point matter that much? I don't think so. Conversely, I've been ahead and unsure how I got there and that often has not worked out so well.

Point number three: Having momentum on your side is also more important than being ahead in the score. Have you ever been ahead 4-0 or better in the first set, let it go to your head and watched it all slip away, helpless to stop it? I have, and it's not an experience I like to repeat. In fact, I almost go out of my way to not start too fast as I know how quickly things can turn. It's much more important to control the momentum of the match than leading in the score. Don't get me wrong; a big lead is a good thing as long as you realize you haven't won anything yet. And of course, if you haven't won anything yet, you haven't lost anything yet, either, so don't be down if all is not well.

I have often had players describe their match this way: "I was up 4-0 and she came back to tie it up 4-4. I was so mad that I let her catch up that I lost the first set and then the match. I usually ask, "If before the match I had told you the score would be 4-4 in the first set, would you be upset?" They are almost always fine with that. Then "Why were you upset when you got to that score?" No answer. The answer could have been "I suddenly became a much better tennis player and 4-0 was just the beginning of an easy victory." No, that didn't happen. It also didn't happen that she was much worse than you thought. So, why be upset at 4-4? And that folks is how you lose momentum. Just as you should not be discouraged if things start badly, you should be wary if they go too well. Nothing is won until all is won.

Thoughts on how to make all this happen

Don't sweat the small stuff: If you are winning easily against a lesser opponent, don't fight over a line call when you are up 5-0. By the same token, if you are down 5-0 and you think you have a chance, don't fight over a line call here either. You will need that energy for your next set comeback.

The other side of the net is not your problem: Observe what's happening on the other side, but try not to get involved. If the line calls are questionable, try to give the benefit of the doubt. If they are horrible, you are on your own. I have never been very good at handling that situation, so I just avoid it and call my own side. Try not to compromise your integrity.

If your opponent is injured, try to play normally rather than take advantage of the injury. I do not say this from a sportsmanship perspective, but rather to avoid screwing up your own game as you try to take advantage of the injury. Do not invest your mental energy in your opponent's problem. Most importantly, if they suggest they can't continue, don't rush up to shake their hand and say "Nice Match." You might just antagonize them enough to continue. Walk up very slowly and say "Nice Match" as you extend your hand. Never, never, never, ever say "Are you sure?" or "Don't quit." Sure as I am writing this, your concentration has been critically compromised and you may hear for years how this great comeback occurred on one leg, all cramped up, or in a daze, all at your expense. After you shake hands you may be as sympathetic and helpful as the situation warrants. *I'm not kidding about this. Trust me.*

All points are important, but some are more important than others. Tiebreakers are nerve wracking. Why? Because each point counts and you only need seven to win or lose. Understandably, these take a lot of mental energy.

Can anyone tell me why, when the score is 5-1, 15-0, that someone loses their temper over an easy miss? Is 5-1, 15-15 a much worse place to be? Yet time and again, this is what I see. Each and every point is not life and death, and we don't have the energy to treat them as such.

4-4, 40-40 requires your full concentration. If you've treated every point up to this point as crucial, you may have no energy reserve when the points really matter.

When the point is over, learn what can be learned from it and then let it go. Do not let it linger. No future points should be lost because of some bonehead mistake you made two points ago. Let it fly away, like a feather in the wind.

When your opponent hits a great serve or a winner, say "Nice Shot." When your opponent hits a decent serve or shot which you do not return, say "Nice Shot." When your opponent hits a 10 MPH serve and you hit it into the bottom of the net, say "Nice Shot." Do you believe it? Of course not. But it's better than calling yourself a "@#$^\$%\$# \$@\$%%@. I think it's a good way to forgive yourself and move on.

In the end you have to be true to yourself. Trying to be something you're not also requires mental energy. I am not suggesting you suppress your personality and become as stoic as a Trappist monk. I'm a talker. In doubles I talk to my partner. In singles I talk to spectators. I find conversation keeps my nerves under control. It doesn't hurt that I'm occasionally funny and puts the crowd (it's been a long time since I've played in front of a crowd) on my side. You may be volatile and prone to spontaneous outbursts of interesting invective and creative profanity or you may be quiet as that Trappist monk. Either way, try not to give too much away to your opponent when you get frustrated. Men get angry. Women, and I don't know why, often throw their head back after they miss; and not in that hair flip coquettish way that men find so attractive, but in a violent backward motion as if someone has just grabbed a handful of hair. All these signs let your opponent know that they are getting to you.

The best example of wasting mental energy was recently displayed by Serena Williams in her quest for the Grand Slam at the 2015 U.S. Open. Serena is currently in the enviable position of being by far the best player in women's tennis. It has not always been true, but it is now. Her close competitors of the past have either retired (Henin, Clijsters, Mauresmo) or declined due to injury or illness (Venus and

Azarenka) and the new generation has yet to produce a reliable competitor.

Serena entered the U.S. Open as the heavy favorite for the title and the first women's Grand Slam in 27 years. Of course there was pressure. Unlike the favorites among the men who could conceivably be beaten by a number of players playing great, no such excuse would be available to Serena.

So how did she do? A first round retirement of her opponent took less than an hour. In the second round someone named Kiki Bertens took her to a tiebreaker in the first set (Serena won) and lost 6-3 in the second, better than most people would have guessed and a sign of things to come. In the third round Serena turned what should have been a routine match against Bethanie Mattek-Sands, a journeyman player never ranked higher than 39 in the world, into an ordeal. After losing the first set 6-3, Serena, repeatedly exhorting herself to "Come On," managed to win the second set 7-5 and finally played near her level winning the third set 6-0. What should have been an easy win turned into a physical and mental struggle.

The fourth round was easier than expected as the big hitting young American Madison Keys was not equal to the challenge of Serena and went down easily 6-3, 6-3.

Serena played her sister Venus in the quarterfinals and after a routine 6-2 first set, lost in the second 6-1, and had to struggle to a 6-3 third set. It is never easy for her to play Venus, and this was no exception. After Flavia Pennetta upset #2 seed Simona Halep in the semi-finals, the only obstacles for Serena were two Italian women, Pennetta and Roberta Vinci, neither of whom had ever won a match from her. The Grand Slam was hers for the taking, adding even more pressure.

In the semi-finals against Vinci, Serena won the first set as expected 6-2. Then the unexpected happened. Every missed shot by Serena was followed by some sign of dismay. Every long point lost was an emotional loss. Losing a close 6-4 set was even more unsettling. For Serena, every set lost against Vinci can be considered close because Vinci's serve is easily handled by Serena and Serena's serve is the best in the world. The third set totally drained Serena as she could not find the energy to perform at a reasonable level. She didn't need a great performance, but she couldn't even find mediocre as the third set was filled with unforced errors on her part. When serving at 3-5 to stay in the match she couldn't reach 90 MPH on her serve when she had been averaging 110 in her match with Venus.

Yes, Vinci hit some very nice half-volleys in the last game. Yes, Vinci took advantage of the opportunity Serena offered, but the drama that Serena injected into the entire tournament took its toll and she had absolutely nothing to give when she needed it most. She looked relieved when it was finally over, like a little girl yelling "Mommy, make it stop, make it stop." Finally it stopped.

Throughout the tournament, Serena threw away opportunities to cruise into the semifinals, mentally and physically fresh. She did not have the mental energy necessary to overcome the nerves and pressure that everyone knew would be coming if she got this close to the Grand Slam.

This was not a totally unpredictable result, and had she dodged the bullet in the semis, there was no guarantee she would survive the finals. Vinci and Pennetta were veterans who, if offered a chance to win a Grand Slam, were going to take full advantage, and they did.

CHAPTER THREE

Anticipation

Anticipation - 1. realization in advance 2. Expectation or hope
3. Intuition, foreknowledge or prescience

World #1 female Caroline Wozniaki was playing former U.S. Open champion Svetlana Kuznetsova in the 4th round of the 2011 U.S. Open. (You'd think I could have chosen an example with easier names!) Midway through the match, in the middle of a great point, Kuznetsova hit a short wide ball to Wozniacki's forehand and came to the net. And that's when it happened - a great example of anticipation in tennis. Wozniacki attempted to pass the perfectly positioned Kuznetsova with a sharp, though high crosscourt forehand which Kuznetsova lunged high and wide and volleyed into the open court for a winner.

Great anticipation? No, it wasn't Kuznetsova who anticipated so well. She simply positioned herself properly and waited for Wozniacki to hit the ball. It was I who showed great anticipation when, as I foresaw, both Patrick McEnroe and Chris Evert heaped lavish praise on Kuznetsova for anticipating Wozniacki's shot direction. Chris Evert pointed out that Kuznetsova played a lot of doubles and acquired her net anticipation from that. McEnroe was less specific, but still overwhelming in his praise.

The video clearly shows Kuznetsova waiting until the ball is struck before moving to finish off the volley. Why would she do otherwise? Her previous shot had forced Wozniacki off the court where she had to hit a winner and the ball she was hitting was no easy sitter. In fact, the only way Kuznetsova can lose this point is by Wozniacki hitting a great passing shot off a difficult ball. Of course, she could guess (Oh I'm sorry, I meant anticipate!) which side Wozniacki would attempt her passing shot and eliminate one side of the court but that would mean she just reduced her chances of making the winning volley to 50% when I estimated they were at least 80 - 90 % . No smart player would do that.

So what's my point? Is this just some curmudgeonly rant by some unknown tennis pro trying to show up two world class tennis players? After all, Chris Evert is remembered as one of the smartest players of her day and Patrick McEnroe is a former Davis Cup Captain and head of USTA Player development.

My point is this; every time a player makes an outstanding stretch volley the announcers rave about his anticipation even when the slow motion replay reveals no such thing. Tennis players within earshot of this telecast or others making similar claims will bemoan their own inability to anticipate. In the modern game, fewer players approach the net, making these falsehoods less likely than in the past, but still, average players think they are in some way deficient in their ability to fathom the mind and body of their opponents.

Let's review the above definitions of Anticipation.

1. *Realization in advance* - This sounds a lot like seeing the future and is beyond my capabilities and probably beyond yours.

2. *Expectation or hope* - Really sounds like guessing to me. There are situations where we can reasonably expect certain results. Lob over your opponent forcing him to turn his back and chase the ball and you can reasonably expect him to lob it back. Hope that he tries a 'tweener (between the legs), but expect the lob.

If your opponent must reach behind himself to get the ball, it is very difficult to hit a crosscourt so make sure you cover the line. Just remember difficult does not mean impossible. Guessing is appropriate in desperate situations, the kind where if we stay where we are we will surely lose the point. Example: Your opponent is five feet from the net with an easy ball above his shoulders. If you don't guess where his shot is going you have no chance to catch up to it. Guess. You will be wrong or overwhelmed 98% of the time in a situation where you should lose 100% of the time. Once in a blue moon you will guess right, get a ball you can handle and win the point. Rarely, but it happens. And when it does, it seems to occur on an important point, sometimes deciding the match. So, when you have nothing to lose, guess.

3. Intuition, foreknowledge or prescience - If you know that Federer hits his forehand passing shots cross court or that Djokovic loves his down the line backhand pass or that Marty the Saturday morning lobber opens up his shoulders to go crosscourt on his forehand, you have some foreknowledge of what is about to happen. With the possible exception of Marty on Saturday, I doubt that this is true.

There are exceptions. Jimmy Connors vs. Dick Stockton - WCT Finals - Dallas - late 1970s. Stockton had played Connors since they were kids. Somewhere along the way he figured out that in pressure situations, Jimmy hit his overhead crosscourt to his opponent's right handed backhand. Deeper and deeper into this very competitive match Stockton lobbed more and more and Connors hit his overhead time and again to the backhand where Stockton was waiting to lob again or pass Connors. It was a classic example of foreknowledge and may have been the difference in Stockton upsetting Connors that day.

Examine your own game and the games of your frequent opponents. Do you always hit the same shot in a certain situation, particularly under pressure? I know I do although I will never tell you which ones. Do your opponents? I once played a very crafty player who seemingly defied logic by winning with no serve, no backhand and no volley. He had a good forehand and a very good lob. He served 95% of the time to your backhand except when the score was 40-0 or 0-40. Far more often than I'm sure even he imagined, he chose to serve to the forehand. Whatever the logic, it made sense to him to mix it up when he was way up or way down. Play him once, it might not be obvious. Play him ten times and you could load up on your forehand in those 40-0 situations.

Let's review. In most situations you don't know what your opponent is going to do with the ball and most of the time you don't need to know. Play good position tennis and wait for her to hit the ball. Anything else is usually just guessing and hurts your cause more than helps it. As noted above, there are exceptions.

Desperate situations require desperate measures. Guess and hope you get lucky. Sometimes inside knowledge of your opponent can lead you in directions others cannot see. Maybe then Chris Evert or Patrick McEnroe can legitimately talk about your great anticipation the next time they announce your match.

CHAPTER FOUR

The Old Bull and the Young Bull

There is a joke about an old bull and a young bull at the top of a hill that I think perfectly illustrates the problem with most players' approach shots. Unfortunately, the story is a bit, what's the word?, off-color, so I can't use it in most of my teaching clinics as I might offend the more prim and proper among you.

Yes, but it's my book and you already bought it, so what the hell?
Two bulls standing at the top of the hill, a young one and an old one. Overlooking the herd of cows below the young bull exclaims, "Why don't we run down there and screw one of them?" The old bull calmly replies, "Why don't we walk down there and screw 'em all?"
And that, ladies and gentlemen is the problem with most people's approach shots!

We see a short ball, run to the ball and then prepare the racquet as if we had no idea when we left that we were actually going to have to hit it. Our feet are too fast for our racquet. It's like the quick, young point guard in basketball who's faster than anyone else on the court, but often forgets that he has to take the basketball with him.

With most approach shots, preparation is far more important than speed. Your racquet should be prepared with your first step towards the ball, high preparation for high balls, low preparation for lower balls. This ensures you can hit the ball in front of you. Most missed approaches are a result of hitting too late or swinging too fast because you have too much to do when you arrive at the ball. Early preparation avoids these mistakes. Also, whether you intend to hit the ball flat, with topspin or with underspin, there's no need to disguise your intent. The only approach you need to disguise is the drop shot approach, as the key is to not make it too easy for your opponent to get to the ball.

Like I said, the slow, old bull knows exactly what he is doing.

CHAPTER FIVE

P. T. S. D.

Yes, it stands for Post Traumatic Stress Disorder. It's a catchy name for a particular playing situation. Let's start with the T for trauma. In this special situation Trauma is defined as:

1) A well hit ball that sends you scrambling wide to retrieve it

2) A ball that hits the tape and proceeds into your backcourt

In the first situation the Post Traumatic Stress is when your opponent, after hitting that good, wide ball mistakenly or ill-advisedly doesn't send you scrambling to the other corner, but rather hits the ball down the middle. The stress is what your tennis brain feels when it realizes this is not as it should be. In fact, it's a lot easier than it should be. "I should go for a winner!" it says. That's the Disorder part. Don't go for a winner. You are not prepared to go for a winner. Your timing is all messed up and you are way more likely to make an error. Hit a safe forcing shot and hit a winner in rhythm when the opportunity presents itself.

The second situation is similar to the first. The ball hits the tape and bounces into the backcourt slower and easier than you expected. Once again your brain says "I should go for a winner"(the undisciplined brain says that a lot!). You should not and for the same reason as situation 1. Your timing is compromised and errors are far more likely than it appears. I know this is counter-intuitive and if John McEnroe were commenting on your match he would be yelling at you to "GO FOR IT." He would be wrong.

Do not confuse this situation with the ball that hits the tape, sits up inside the service line and begs like a dog smelling bacon to be hit for a winner. Real easy is real easy and I am not suggesting you waste these opportunities.

I know how hard it is to change your perception of these situations. Until now, no one ever made you aware that this situation even existed. You may still not notice these situations until you miss your attempted winner. Then you'll think to yourself that that old guy in Buffalo isn't as full of s--t as I thought he was. Don't feel bad. Somehow, I will know your sentiment and take comfort in that.

Watch the pros on TV. When this situation occurs, and the pro misses, you'll now know why. Of course, they don't always miss. But it happens more than you'd imagine.

CHAPTER SIX

Random Thoughts on Doubles

When choosing a partner, there are few rules. Some partners are best friends, while other successful teams barely speak on the court and less off it. Some teams thrive with contrasting styles, one player a good server and/or big hitter while the other player sets things up with placement and finesse. Some good teams have players who are exactly alike. I knew one team that was successful, in part, because they both looked like the two most unlikely good tennis players you could imagine, each unlikely in their own way, of course. You can never be sure until you play together.

This next part I believe to be crucial. Most teams have an "A" and a "B" player. This is not about who is better. The "A" player likes to strategize and be in charge, while the "B" player doesn't mind the "A" player taking control. Two "A" players are OK if they each respect one another and can work things out. Two "B" players is not the way to go. You need someone in charge and neither one of the "B's" wants to fill that role. Before you ask, you know who you are. Also, some players are better with a partner who is better than they are. Some don't like the pressure of being the stronger player, just as some don't like being the weaker one.

Which side you should play also has no rules. At better levels, it is all about returning serve. Which setup gives your team the best service returns and thus the best chance to break serve? At lower levels, it often means covering up a weakness or weaknesses, like a bad backhand. Experiment and see how it goes.

My only rule is that on an unbalanced team, one player definitely stronger than the other, I want the weaker player on his best, most confident side, because if he does not perform well, we won't win.

These are my remaining thoughts on doubles:

1. Show up on time, or even better, go to the match together if possible. Waiting for your partner to arrive is unnerving and distracts from your pre-match preparation.

2. You win and lose as a team. I cannot emphasize this too much. If your partner is having a bad day, you must pick up the slack. If you cannot, you are as responsible for the loss as she is. In other words, we win and lose as a team. Got it?

3. Don't take anything you hear personally, from your partner or your opponents. If your partner tells you to move your fat ass (I, of course would be more diplomatic with my partner) she is just encouraging you to be a little more aggressive. Some players respond to positive encouragement while others need a little more aggressive motivation. Remember that your partner only wants what you want and that, is a WIN.

4. Pay attention in the warmup. You might learn something. If you do, don't be afraid to share it. Tell your partner what you see, as in, "looks like she has a good forehand, but her volley is weak."

5. HAVE A PLAN!!! If it's outside, who serves with the wind or into the sun? Do we come to the net a lot, or stay back? Who's got the better overhead? Are we going to poach a lot, or almost never? Create a basic game plan and adjust as necessary.

6. Doubles is a cross-court game. For better or worse, down the line shots tend to end the point, usually for the worse. Almost all down the line shots involve taking a cross-court shot and changing the direction of the return. This is inherently harder than hitting it back in the direction it came, particularly if the ball is hit hard.

7. When in doubt, lob.

8. Try not to lob when running forward. Despite your fine sense of touch, it is likely to go long. The momentum of you running forward is enough to send the ball flying, even if you "barely touched it."

9. If it's good for one, it's good for both. If your partner runs back to chase a lob, you should probably be moving back as well. The more difficult the lob, the further back you should go. Conversely, if your partner hits a shot that he follows to the net, you should probably be going with him.

10. Balance the court. If your partner goes wide off the court, move to the middle. If she goes too close to the net, back up to protect against the lob. As they return to a better position, so can you.

11. If you are in the same spot you were in two shots ago and you haven't hit the ball, you are spectating and not playing.

12. Net players are to be avoided, unless you are attacking them.

13. There are not a lot of holes in doubles. Threading the needle to hit a winner is a losing strategy. Don't be afraid to hit the ball at people. When you have created a hole, take full advantage.

14. When struggling, don't be afraid to change formations. If you are struggling returning serve, play both players back. If necessary, play both players back when serving if your serve isn't good enough to keep your partner at the net from being attacked. Use the Australian formation if your opponents are too comfortable returning cross court. None of these suggestions need to be permanent. Often, a switch for a game or two can be disruptive or even decisive.

15. Whether things start well or poorly, they may change and often do. Be prepared when it happens.

16. Pay attention to what works and what doesn't. This does not mean that you should exploit a weakness to the exclusion of all else. What if they find a solution to that problem? What do you do then?

I prefer to attack the weakness selectively, when I need a point, not just on every point.

17. You win and lose as a team!

18. The Shrimp Rule. If I am coaching your USTA team, unhealthy post-match snacks are better, but shrimp is always best.

CHAPTER SEVEN

Random Thoughts on Mixed Doubles (Not a Fan)

I am not good at mixed doubles. Never have been, never will be. In my day (doesn't that make me sound ancient?) there really was only one good reason to play mixed doubles. Let's call it "love." Anything else was just bad for your tennis. Occasionally teaching pros would play with young female students, but that was about it. Other good players, except for the aforementioned reason, never went near it.

I think there were many reasons why we felt the way we did about Mixed. First and foremost, the women usually weren't strong enough to compete with the men. I think technology has changed that quite a bit. Now women, particularly with their groundstrokes, can hit the ball as hard as men. The lighter, stronger racquets are part of that reason. More and better female players is the other part.

Secondly, we played open events where we couldn't avoid the very scary situation of playing against a woman or team that really doesn't belong on the court with you, and you end up, despite your best efforts not to, hitting the woman with an overhead or something. It just wasn't good for your reputation.

And the final reason, and I'm not sure why this is true, and still true, is that mixed doubles attracts a lot of jerky guys: guys who are abusive to their wives, guys trying to impress someone (who? Their partner? going about it the wrong way!) and guys who hit the ball too hard for their skill level and inevitably hit someone with an out of control shot. Often, the victim is their own partner getting a too hard, out of control first serve in the back of the head or the middle of the back. Who wants to be on court for that? Worse, he whacks your partner unnecessarily and now you have to kinda retaliate. The best at this was a friend of mine who was as polite as a young man could be. Hit his partner and he would never stoop to hitting yours, but I guarantee you would leave the court bruised.

I'm glad I got all that out, I feel much better already as I give you my thoughts on mixed doubles play.

1. The Universal Truth of mixed doubles is that the women win it, and the men lose it. This assumes that the man is the stronger player. The strategy in mixed, in a phrase is, hit the ball at the woman. This means the guys see fewer shots and have fewer opportunities to do something positive with the ball. In a losing match, they almost never do enough with the balls they get, either by trying to do too much and missing, or by just keeping the ball in play and leaving the woman open to attack. The woman who manages to hold up under this barrage is usually on the winning team.

2. As in all unbalanced doubles situations, the weaker player needs to be comfortable and therefore should get first preference as to which side she is to receive on. This also applies to serving when outside. If given the choice, try to arrange the serving rotation so that the weaker partner is serving where they are most comfortable; favorable sun and wind.

3. Mixed should not be about holding or breaking the guys' serves. Holding serve for the man should be a given. It's about getting your partner to hold while breaking the other woman. I often hear about receiving strategies based on how we can break the other guy to the detriment of breaking the other woman. "He had a good slice serve, so I played the deuce court" is not a good reason as to why you played that side. You probably aren't going to break him anyway. Concentrate on the one in the skirt.

34

4. I hate mixed doubles teams where the guy tries to play 90% of the court and the woman lets him, even if it's a winning strategy. However, women may defer to their partner when it comes to put away shots such as overheads. This does not mean all overheads, just those in the middle or the high, hit off the bounce types.

5. Guys playing mixed love to poach and surprisingly, some are pretty good at it. If you or your partner can't figure out the guy at the net, just go over his head. Why play the guessing game?

6. Guys: Be careful about taking a ball off your partner's racquet. Remember Rule #1. If she loses confidence, you lose the match. She may not say anything. She may just give you "The Look." For all you guys who are married, I don't need to describe it. For those of you who aren't, I have no words to describe it.

7. Communication is important but conferences after every point slow play down to a crawl. Keep it short. Discussing general strategy, like whether to poach frequently or not against one or the other, can be done on the crossovers.

8. Communication is important. High fives are occasionally acceptable. No Kissing.

9. You know how couples often tell you they have a rule "No going to bed angry"? That's what they say, but I never believe them, but anyway…. try not to leave the court mad at your partner. I've taken that long, silent drive home. Never once did I enjoy it.

CHAPTER EIGHT

Cheating

Don't cheat! That was easy. Oh, you weren't asking if you should cheat, were you?

Unfortunately, every so often you encounter an opponent who cheats, not someone who is a bad line caller, but someone who cheats. I have no definitive advice for this situation as nothing has ever worked for me. Paramount to any action you may take is the effect it will have on your own game. If you become distracted and it negatively affects your play, the cheater is likely to win even if he never cheats again.

Possible solutions and potential drawbacks include:

The threat of physical violence - Can you back that up?

Calling for a line judge - Most line judges hate to overrule calls and when they do, it is usually against you.

Retaliatory cheating - Besides the moral dilemma, are you ready for the war that follows?

Serenity - You call your side, he calls his. Downside includes losing unfairly. Upside is you can sleep like a baby.

A corollary to the cheater is the person who tries to influence your calls either with out and out accusations "That ball was in!" or the more furtive "Are you sure?" Sometimes it's just a long look at the line or something along the lines of "Did you call that out?"

At some point you might suggest that the rules require you to call your side and for her to call her side, end of story.

If that turns discontent into cheating, see solutions above.

CHAPTER NINE

No Excuses

As you must know by now, the results speak for themselves. There are no excuses. You win because you were better, you lose because your opponent was. No one is interested in hearing "it doesn't really count because …" If you played, you were healthy. If you were sick or injured, you didn't play. End of Story. My favorite excuse is, and always will be, "I played bad!" Anyone can win when they play well, when your opponent puts the ball in the middle of the court and let's you do whatever you want with it. Under such circumstances I am undefeated. Besides, what makes you think your opponent doesn't have a boatload of similar excuses if she loses. Can you win when you aren't playing your best? I don't know about you, but I play my best tennis once or twice a season. The rest of the time, it's a struggle.

That's what makes it so much fun!

I repeat, There are no Excuses!!! …….

but there are…

Extenuating Circumstances

Extenuating circumstances are not excuses. I stand wholeheartedly by what I said above, there are no excuses. Extenuating circumstances are reasons for losing that may no longer exist. Losing 6-1, 6-1 does not leave a lot of hope for future encounters with the same opponent and as Andy Dufresne says in "The Shawshank Redemption": "Hope is a good thing, maybe the best of things." So where is my hope for a future encounter? It lies in "extenuating circumstances." Your child was feeling sick when you left the house and you were worried. Six hours moving a truckload of dirt did nothing for your pre-game preparation. A fender bender in the parking lot rattled your nerves. These and many others like them are all one time events that, with a little preparation and a little luck, won't exist in your next encounter. I've read that the top pros (Agassi, Sampras et al.) always have extenuating circumstances in their losses. I suppose it's easier to face Andy Roddick's 140 mph serve again if you believe there was a good reason you didn't return it the first time.

If Sampras and Agassi need some extenuating circumstances, I think it's OK for us to have them once in a while.

CHAPTER TEN

Observation: Line Judges

Has anyone noticed how accurate line judges are proven to be by the Hawkeye system? Balls served 120 MPH near the lines are time and again challenged by the players and time and again the lines people are proven correct. When their call is overruled, it's often because a mere sliver of the ball has or hasn't grazed the line. You might also keep in mind that not even Hawkeye is 100% accurate, although everyone has agreed to accept it as if it is.

Unlike other sports where instant replay is used, tennis' system is conclusive. No players, coaches or announcers question the results. Other sports replay systems are often inconclusive or even worse, produce results that seem to fly in the face of the visual evidence.

So if the lines people are so good, and the system so accurate, why in the world was the umpire in the 2015 U.S. Open's Men's Final overruling calls over and over again? Eva Asderaki-Moore, the first woman to umpire a U.S. Open Men's final, correctly overruled three calls missed by the lines person and was proven correct in all three instances. Hawkeye kept this from becoming the kind of match that John McEnroe or Ilya Nastase would have thrived in, revving up the boisterous full house crowd into a mob.

I don't think Federer or Djokovic would have enjoyed that kind of atmosphere. Fortunately, with the competent people and systems tennis has in place, those days are unlikely to return.

Just one more thought. If John McEnroe had played in this era, his tennis genius would have been even more appreciated, as it wouldn't have been often overshadowed by his juvenile, boorish, bratty tirades on court. Just a thought.

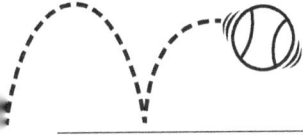

CHAPTER ELEVEN

Two types of teaching basics

Beginners in almost all sports are taught the same way, whether they hope to play in a recreational setting or be at the top of their sport. While that is true of tennis also, it's not true for very long. Once we get past the stage of making contact with the ball and keeping it somewhere near the court, teaching paths start to differentiate. I don't know if this is true in very many other sports. In basketball, dribbling is dribbling and a jump shot is a jump shot. In baseball, hitting a pitched ball is a very difficult thing, but it is equally difficult for Major Leaguers as well as Little Leaguers. It does not vary with the age or skill level of the group as long as they have the necessary strength to handle the equipment.

This is not true in tennis. Perhaps it is because it is a sport that attracts a lot of adult beginners, but that is only partly the reason.

Modern tennis has advanced rapidly. The top players of today play the game at a very much higher level than past generations. The improved equipment has played a large role. Today's players use racquets with larger and more forgiving hitting areas and the strings allow for much greater spin and control than in the past. Competition has also played a huge role in producing players that are bigger, stronger, faster and more skilled than those of earlier generations, and to succeed they have learned to play "the Modern Game."

The "Classic Game" consisted of one-handed backhands, often or only sliced, flat forehands sometimes hit with topspin and players who often went into the net and sometimes went in at every possible opportunity.

The "Modern Game" consists of powerful forehands hit with semi-western or western grips (I'll explain shortly) and hit at every opportunity from every position on the court. This means that almost any ball that can be hit with a forehand is hit with a forehand, whether on the forehand or backhand side of the court. Backhands are almost always two-handed and are hit with topspin. The one-handed backhands out there have to be just as aggressive as the two-handed. Power is generated from rotational energy as players coil and uncoil their bodies as their arms swing through the shot. Players control and spin the ball so well from either side that modern players don't venture into the net nearly as often as players from the past. No one invented or dictated all of this; it just came to pass as players experimented with the newer equipment and learned what they could and couldn't do. Just to get a feel for the difference, go to Youtube and look at an old match from the Connors-McEnroe era. You'll soon be looking for the fast forward button because it seems to be in slow motion. I assure you it is not. That's just the speed at which it was played.

Injuries in the old days consisted of tennis elbow, the occasional shoulder injury and the usual knee and ankle injuries caused by missteps of one kind or another.

Modern players also injure their knees and ankles, but now they also injure wrists hitting massive amounts of topspin. The rotational energy generated now creates hip problems and abdominal strains. No one I started playing with ever complained of a stomach muscle strain or a hip problem. Now it is fairly common.

For those that are taught the modern game, the sky is the limit. With enough athleticism, hard work and perseverance, Wimbledon or a Division I scholarship is a possibility.

Modern players use a western or semi-western grip. A western or semi-western grip (holding the racquet with your palm facing up) makes it easier to hit topspin and create more power as you move your wrist to present a flat racquet face to the ball. This is all very nice, but western grips make low balls difficult and also keep the racquet face in line with the ball for a much shorter period of time. This makes many shots easier to hit hard and with lots of topspin but make it more difficult to handle low shots. Rotating your body as you drive through the ball requires a higher degree of precision and thus more perfect timing. The only way I know how to get that kind of timing is to hit a lot (did I say a lot? I meant a ton) of balls. Are you prepared to do that?

Speed is very important in modern tennis. The ball is flying across the net faster than ever. Getting to the ball early helps avoid those troublesome low balls and allows you to comfortably reach the ball with your two-handed backhand.

In the Classic game you can still hit hard and with topspin but less so than those guys on TV. By keeping the physics simpler, you don't have to be as precise when you hit the ball. Low balls are a little easier to deal with making speed less of an issue. Speed is always important, but less so.

So here is the modern teaching pro's dilemma. Once you have demonstrated the ability to contact the ball on the strings and I have your personal history and future goals, what type of game should I teach you?

If I teach you the modern game and you decide to become just a casual player, will those severe grips and rotational strokes be too hard for you to time? And if I don't teach you the modern game, will you not reach your competitive potential because your strokes are stuck in the 1970s?

Fortunately, the decision making on my part is not as hard as it might be. Most kids want to hold the racquet with a semi-western grip anyway and since their potential knows few limits, I give them all a chance to be stars.

Adults are a different story, but here again it's easier than it looks. In shape, reasonably young, athletic adults also have a big upside so let's not limit them early on.

Most adults I get aren't so young or athletic or in shape and so once again the choice is fairly easy. The Classic game gets them playing enjoyable tennis much sooner and is less demanding on their bodies.

If these decisions are so easy, why did I bother to write this?

Consider this a warning. Tennis pros who have grown up in this Millennium only know the Modern Game. Too many of them teach only that to too many of their students. It may make the game more frustrating than it needs to be as well as produce more physical breakdowns. They may not recognize that the only way most of us will get to the U.S. Open is to take the #7 train to Flushing Meadow. One pro I know shouts every year that he hates the U.S. Open. At its conclusion, too many people want him to teach them to hit the ball just like Federer or Djokovic or worse yet, Rafael Nadal. Every fall he must explain why that is not possible.

CHAPTER TWELVE

Teaching Lassie to Bark

Teaching is a wonderful profession. It is a great feeling to help someone achieve their goals and an even better feeling when years later they tell you how much they enjoyed your class or how much you helped them or even changed their lives. The icing on the cake is that almost never will you hear how much you confused them, belittled them or changed their lives in a negative way. I told you this was a wonderful profession!

I teach tennis full-time and while it is rare for an English teacher to take credit for her former student's latest novel, tennis pros do it all the time. "My student is ranked 3rd in the East, my kid got a scholarship to a Division I school etc., etc.

Don't misunderstand me, I think teaching tennis is as noble a profession as teaching most other things but let's look at what it takes to make a very good junior player, let alone a professional.
The first ingredient is a good athlete. He/she doesn't have to be a great athlete, but it helps if you have a good one.

The second ingredient is a committed athlete. Is he willing to do what it takes to achieve excellence? That usually means tennis after school every day and tournaments or matches on weekends. Since most of these kids come from families where academics are important, it means doing all this while maintaining good grades. You often find kids doing homework before their tennis classes or in between matches at tournaments. Friday is often a travel day so there is makeup work for time missed from school. This doesn't leave a lot of time for "hanging out" with their friends.

In tennis you have to have good practice partners, so that means practicing with your competition. Since everyone wants to "play up" this often means getting beaten by kids who are better than you, if only because they are older. No one likes losing.

The third ingredient is a committed family. Parents who are willing to get their kid to the tennis center every day, pay for the classes, private lessons, court time, equipment and tournament expenses are not your everyday Mom and Pop. Even if the parents are committed, often that commitment is overridden by other family commitments, financial or otherwise.

So you have an athletic kid, committed to excellence with parents who are willing to follow the dream. Any Pro worth that designation should be able to guide this kid to a sectional ranking or better. Sure, things happen. A player gets injured, discovers the opposite sex, can't handle the competing or gets turned off by the pressure of unrealistic expectations, his own or others. A smart Pro can help keep all these things under control but as far as the nuts and bolts and Xs and Os of the game, it's almost as easy as teaching Lassie to bark.

Unfortunately, these are the kids that Pros use to build their reputations. Jimmy Arias, who reached the #5 in the world ranking was coached by his father Tony until he left Buffalo for Nick Bolletieri's Tennis Academy in Florida. Jimmy arrived in Florida with an amazing forehand, mediocre backhand, mediocre serve and no volley. A few years later he left Bolletieri's with an Amazing forehand, mediocre backhand and serve and no volley. He rode that great forehand to the semis of the US Open where Nick was more than happy to tell you the great contribution he had made to Jimmy's game. The Pros in Buffalo were no country bumpkins either. Many of them were just as happy to tell you how much they helped Jimmy. I guess father Tony's contributions weren't that important.

The moral of the story is to find a decent Pro, someone you and your kid like, someone you trust, and let him lead the way. He will not be the difference between your kid on the Pro circuit or not. He will not be the difference between a Division I scholarship or not, but he might be the person to help get you to the finish line, wherever that might be, and to enjoy the race along the way.

Ironically, driven by the dream as parent and/or child are, I can't believe they will follow this advice beyond the first bump in the road. You see, there is someone out there who says he can teach Lassie to sing!

CHAPTER THIRTEEN

We Are Who We Are

When you hand a person a tennis racquet for the very first time, the way they grab it tells you something about how this is going to go. Some grab it as if they are shaking hands (Eastern grip), some grab it with their hand on top (Continental grip), and a few grab it from underneath (Western grip). Let them attempt to hit a few balls and you start to understand how their brains work.

I say this to illustrate how we are all different with unique brains. Some of us intuit the easy way to do things, some of us insist on doing it the hard way. Some are adaptable and some are not.

Every time I watch a pro player struggle with a particular stroke on TV, I know there are thousands of fans and hundreds of tennis pros shouting about how they could have taught this person to hit the ball better than that. But could they?

Remember, no one gets to be on TV without being a great athlete, and you don't get to be a great tennis player without lots of excellent instruction (OK, so maybe a few break this rule, but not many, and not in the last 20 years). So what accounts for this phenomenon?

Richard Gasquet has arguably the best one-handed backhand on the tour. He also has the worst forehand, far and away, among the top thirty players in the world. His backhand coach didn't know how to teach forehands? I doubt it.

Coincidentally, Stefan Edberg had the best backhand of his generation and a forehand that could charitably be described as "almost mediocre." Was it his coach as well, who couldn't teach forehands? Elena Dementieva had fantastic groundstrokes with a serve that couldn't survive a 4.0 ladies USTA match. Every serve looked like it was her first one. She had no confidence and no clue. The Russians don't know how to teach the serve?

Everyone's brain works differently. Each of us has things we find easy, and each of us has other things that we think are hard. I am good with numbers and terrible with mechanical things. My doubles partner has an excellent legal mind but can't figure out how to make his lawnmower work (or so he says).

Gasquet and Edberg were born to hit backhands. The forehand for them has always been a lot of work. I'm sure they've practiced more on the forehand side than the backhand, but will never be more comfortable on that side.

Dementieva has probably served until her arm fell off, but that's not going to make it feel natural and confident. She's just not wired that way.

John McEnroe – Great serve, exquisite volley, good backhand, funky forehand

Ivan Lendl – Powerful serve and groundstrokes, no feel whatsoever on the volley. That's why he never won Wimbledon

Jimmy Connors – Great groundstrokes, excellent volleyer, very ordinary mechanical serve

All three, multiple Grand Slam winners, yet all three had different, but obvious weaknesses.

So the next time you watch a decent junior or club player hit, please don't be too hard on the instructor when you see a stroke that doesn't look right. I've had several people through the years who just could not figure out how to stroke the ball as I wished. They tried and I tried but it was just not meant to be.

One of my favorite lines is to tell another pro that if he can teach John X to hit a good Y(whatever the stroke is), he's a better instructor than I am. Fortuantely for my ego, no one's been able to pull it off.

We are who we are.

CHAPTER FOURTEEN

Strengths and Weaknesses

As I said in the last chapter, we are who we are and not much can change that. This does not mean that if your backhand is your least comfortable stroke that it cannot get better, just that it probably will remain your least comfortable stroke.

So that's your weakness. What can we do about it? The more you practice, the better it will get, but how much better, and what about the rest of your game?

My flat backhand and my backhand passing shot have always been the weakest part of my game. Attack my backhand and you are likely to be successful. I've practiced and practiced those shots but reality says they aren't going to get much better, particularly under pressure.

I have a much better forehand, and a good serve and volley.

Through the years I have had some very good wins against players as good as me and a few definitely better than me. In all those wins I can never remember coming off the court and saying I won because my backhand passing shot was really good today. I won because my good shots were very good, not that my weaknesses had been better. Of course, if I could, I did not expose my weaknesses any more than I absolutely had to.

At some point you have to accept who you are and build your game around that. Not everyone can be "An all-around player" nor do we all need to be.

Malcolm Gladwell, in his book "David and Goliath" talks about a coach of a 12 year old girls team who focused only on defense when he realized that he could not make his girls decent offensive players. He bet it all on the only strength he had. Extreme, but effective. You can do the same.

If you spend too much practice time on your weaknesses, you may lose the advantage you have with your strengths. Focusing on what you do well can also keep your confidence level high.

My best doubles win came with a partner just like me; good serve and net game, lousy service return. Our mantra was to not miss volleys and overheads, no double faults and every serve we managed to get back was a bonus. It worked perfectly. Like I said, it was my best doubles win!

Exult in your strengths and don't beat yourself up over your weaknesses. You already know you are going to miss those shots. Focus on what you do well and you might find yourself in the winners circle.

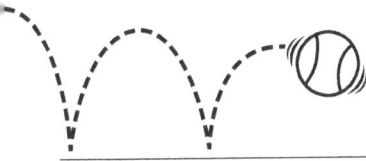

CHAPTER FIFTEEN

The Sons and the Daughters

The most common name in professional sports these days is, you guessed it, "Junior." Whether it's Ken Griffey Jr., Patrick Ewing Jr., or perhaps even with some other name, the NBA, NFL and MLB are filled with the offspring of former players. Sometimes the kids play different sports as in Grant Hill (NBA) son of Calvin Hill (NFL). Tennis player Yannick Noah sired Joachim Noah (NBA), but for the most part the kids, for a variety of reasons, play daddy's sport. Chris Long, #1 NFL draft pick is the son of Hall-of-Famer Howie Long. Joe, "jellybean" Bryant played for the Philadelphia 76ers and is the father of Kobe Bryant. In baseball, Ray Boone was the father of All-Star catcher Bob Boone who is the father of All-Stars Bret and Aaron Boone. Lebron James' son is already being offered college basketball scholarships and he's barely in the eighth grade. The list goes on and on.

Once upon a time professional athletes were professionals because they were athletic and more skilled than the other kids. Now, good coaching and training are everywhere. Almost everyone who aspires to a college scholarship or pro career can develop the skills necessary to keep the dream alive. What seems to separate the men from the boys is the athleticism, and who better to inherit that from than a former professional athlete.

I tell everyone that my son was not a Division I athlete, not because he wasn't good enough, but because I wasn't good enough. There's some truth in that. These days it's hard to be a Division I athlete with Division III genes. The competition today is fierce and often mediocre athletes, no matter how hard they try and how skilled they become, just can't break through.

The reason they often play their father's sport is that their father's athleticism was particularly helpful in that sport. No one would mistake great homerun hitter Cecil Fielder for a great all-round athlete, and we might all have been surprised if his son, Prince Fielder (every bit as rotund as his father) showed up for the decathlon, but he did not. Like his father, Prince has that very rare gift of being able to hit a baseball thrown by a major league pitcher, and to hit that pitch very far. 6'10" basketball players producing 6'8" sons who excel at basketball do not stretch the imagination very far. Rick Barry had four sons who played in the NBA and the fifth played for Division I Kansas. Archie Manning producing quarterbacks as if they grew in his backyard is also something we've come to expect. For this very reason, siblings often share the pro stage.

But not in tennis. Andre Agassi and Steffi Graf have more grand Slam titles than even the Williams sisters and we haven't heard a peep from the USTA about the future talents of their offspring. The same is true of Jimmy Connors and John McEnroe. Nothing from Chris Evert or Tracy Austin either.

The phenomenon is not limited to the USA. European stars are no better at producing world class offspring. And the Australians, who love the sport like no other country, do not have a Newcombe or Laver or Rosewall amongst their current crop of budding stars.
In fact there is currently only one player in the top 100 whose parent was also in the top 100, Edouard Roger-Vasselin of France. Recently retired American Taylor Dent is the son of Phil Dent a former top 20 player. That's it.

Why? Why do you think?

Unlike most sports, tennis is very parent intensive. There are very few school programs involving tennis. Parents who wish their kids to get involved have to either teach them themselves or enroll them in a program at the local club.

If they show an interest, there are more programs, lessons, leagues and tournaments to follow. All or most of these will require parental participation, at least for travel and expenses. Top juniors hit balls at least five times a week, and often six or seven. Elite players travel hundreds of miles several times a month to play in tournaments. Often they are the only player from their club, which means a parent travels with them. Court fees and lessons continue; all this adds up to quite a commitment, financial and otherwise.

It takes a special parent or parents to keep the dream alive. Many can't afford the time or expense. Many can't focus on one child to the detriment of his/her siblings. Many just don't want to.
Andy Roddick's parents moved the family from Texas to Florida to help Andy's older brother John's tennis. It turns out John didn't have what it takes, but Andy did. Would you have done that for your son, even if you could? Will Andy?

Former pros could probably manage the travel and expenses necessary to keep their child in the game, but that's just one side of the story.

I think that most parents have no idea what's in store for them when the Head Pro at their club walks over to them and says that their little Brandon/Megan is really quite talented and he/she really likes the sport and may have a future in the game.

After the initial flattery wears off, they begin to realize that they have started down a path which insidiously keeps requiring a little more of their time, attention and cash. Before they know it, they start worrying about ITF (International Tennis Federation) points and hotel rooms in Kalamazoo, MI, home of the Junior Nationals and a ticket to the U. S. Open.

Touring tennis professionals know all about this stuff. They have lived it. Only a minute percentage of them got to the tour any other way. You hear about the big kid who didn't start playing football until he was a senior in high school and now is looking forward to the NFL draft after a successful college career or the NBA prospect who was discovered in Africa and at 6'10" seemed rather coordinated and was brought over here by a coach or scout. This doesn't happen in tennis. Even the players that come from obscure countries like Yannick Noah (Cameroon) and Marcos Baghdatis (Cypress) were trained in tennis countries like France or Spain. Tennis is starting players younger and younger. Hell, they have an 8 and under national tournament now. Soon, the only requirement will be no Huggies allowed.

To his credit, tennis academy guru Nick Bolleteri advises parents to guide their kids to sports like soccer until they are 8 or 9.
Many pros (most,all?) don't look back fondly on this time as the time when they began piling up trophies. I'm sure many see it as a lost childhood, filled with pressure and lacking many experiences that most normal kids get to enjoy.

Andre Agassi famously recounts in his book how he hated his parents' decision to send him to The Bolleteri Tennis Academy in Florida away from his family and friends in Las Vegas. Jennifer Capriati became the sole source of family income when she turned Pro at fourteen. That pressure helped lead her to turn up in a hotel room, stoned, and accused of shoplifting after disappearing for a few days.

Even the Pro Tour is not as glamourous as it appears. Endless travel, endless losses (only ONE player wins a tournament), endless expenses make the tour a tough grind. Let's not forget the training and the inevitable injuries. It's even harder for the women, who may not be as comfortable touring the night life of whatever city they happen to be in. Hard to make friends, even harder to keep them as they are your competitors. John McEnroe broke up the number one doubles team in the world when his partner Peter Fleming started beating him in singles. John felt Peter knew his strengths and weaknesses too well.

For the top few the payoffs are enormous, but even cracking the Top 100 in the entire world is not necessarily a ticket to financial security. And how likely is it that your kid is going to crack the top 100?
Apparently, all this is too high a price for modern pros to pay as parents; too high for them and too high for their children.

But, not to worry, there will always be others chasing the dream, parents and children alike. For many of them, it will all be worth it, no matter what the outcome. For others, you have been warned!

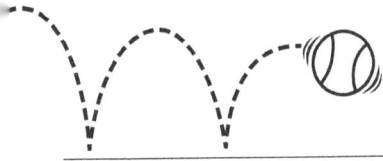

CHAPTER SIXTEEN

Magic, Jason and Roger

Serving a tennis ball and shooting a basketball are similar in the sense that they are skills that can be learned in a relatively short period of time. In other words, the 10,000 hour rule doesn't necessarily apply. For those of you who don't know, the 10,000 hour rule says that it takes approximately 10,000 hours to master complex skills, like composing a symphony or becoming a chess grandmaster.

Serving a tennis ball is also similar to shooting a free throw or a three point shot in basketball. All are done without direct interference from your opponent. In the case of the three point shot, the defense is active, but if you are closely guarded this shot is rarely taken, except in desperate end game situations.

Shooting and serving, while relatively simple skills can both be improved with repetition. Magic Johnson and Jason Kidd entered the NBA after just one season of college and Roger Federer burst onto the tennis scene at about the same age, 19. While Roger was a good server early, Magic and Jason were not good shooters; good defenders and rebounders, great passers, but not good shooters.

Magic came into the league as a decent free throw shooter making about 75-80% of his free throws and an abysmal three point shooter, attempting few and making very few of those, approximately 20%. He eventually became an elite free throw shooter, leading the league one year, and a respectable three point shooter in the 35% range.

Jason Kidd was a 69% free throw shooter who became an 80% free throw shooter. His three point percentage went from the low 20s to as high as 41%.

Even though they were both all-stars early in their careers, they worked on those areas of their games that needed improvement. Over the years, while they lost strength and quickness they improved their skills. Hundreds of thousands of dedicated practice shots improve your shooting. How could it be otherwise?

Roger Federer, on the other hand probably has a jump shot which has not improved much in these last 15 years. Oh, but his serve has. In fact, in a recent interview he asserted as much. While he may be a little older, slower, and with less stamina, the one part of the game that is totally in his control, the serve, has gotten better.

Fed still hits his first serves in the 120+ range. He still hits a high percentage, perhaps now even a higher percentage of his first serves. His placement is impeccable and his second serve is almost as good. As if that wasn't enough, I believe he is better than ever in producing a quality first serve under pressure. I believe the stats on his holding serve bear this out. He is right at the top of the ATP stats in this regard, just behind the giants John Isner and Ivo Karlovic.

When asked what changes we'll see in tennis in the future, I usually respond that the players can't get much bigger and faster or hit the ball much harder but they can improve their first serve percentage. Anytime you have total control over the play, as you do with your serve, and you are only successful 50-60% of the time, there is room for improvement. I think Federer proves this in tennis just like Magic Johnson and Jason Kidd have shown this in basketball.

Maybe that's why they are all Hall-of-Famers.

CHAPTER SEVENTEEN

Observation: What are you afraid of?

I happened to mention Jennifer Capriati when listing the quality women tennis players during the middle part of the decade and a friend mentioned that he had met her while working at a club in Florida. She was starting a tennis academy and was looking to drum up some business.

If you are not familiar with the Capriati story, let me give you a very brief outline. At fourteen, Jennifer was the darling of the tennis world. A big strong girl, she could hit the ball a ton and was skilled well beyond her years. As so many of the very top girls were in those days, she was coached by her father, Stefano. Soon, Jennifer was having success on the tour and moving up the rankings, while racking up many "youngest ever to" records, including youngest ever to reach the "top ten."

As she became more successful she became her family's primary (only?) source of income. After a few years of this, the pressure became too great and Jennifer left the tour and was next heard from as the result of a shoplifting and marijuana charge.

To make a long story less tedious you need to know she came back to the tour, won the Australian Open twice, the French Open once and eventually retired due to some injuries.

I only mention all this because I don't believe she opened her tennis academy and if she did it was short lived. Perhaps it was the shoplifting and marijuana charge that did her in.

But think about it. Who better to empathize with these tennis prodigies and the pressure they were dealing with? Instead of avoiding her because of her history, she could have used it as a cautionary tale for the player and her parents. But not to worry. Every parent says the same thing. "My daughter's fine. She loves tennis. She loves the competition. She's fine."

If it wasn't fine, someone like Jennifer would have been the right person to see through the mask to the problems underneath. Her experience may have made her ideal to be the coach of these kids.

Unfortunately, this story does not end well. Capriati had a near fatal drug overdose which she recovered from and a stalking charge against her from her ex-boyfriend.

This doesn't mean she didn't understand the pressure of tennis. It just means she might not have been the right person to get your kid through it.

CHAPTER EIGHTEEN

High Tech Analysis

You probably know about "Moneyball", Michael Lewis' best seller about the Oakland Athletics and how they competed with a payroll less than a third of the New York Yankees. Through something called advanced metrics, the A's were able to evaluate talent differently (better?) than the rest of the league and successfully competed with players other teams had undervalued. Unfortunately for the Athletics, pro sports tend to emulate success and the advantage they once had has largely disappeared. Through a combination of high tech services such as a pitch by pitch analysis for every game and more analysis for every ball put in play, we now have stats such as "slugging percentage against left-handed fastballs" and "average pitch count per at bat" for every hitter. The data in baseball probably rivals the NSA domestic phone call surveillance analysis with the same problem of "how do I analyze all this stuff?"

The NBA put in sophisticated recording cameras in all there stadia and now each NBA team has their own analytics department trying to figure out how valuable each player is in a fluid game like basketball. This creates some counter-intuitive conclusions that force many coaches and GMs to reevaluate talent. For example, Kyle Korver, perhaps the best three point shooter in the game, makes his team's offense more efficient just by being on the floor. His defender is scared to death to leave him even for a second to help out a teammate and thus his team scores more easily because of the threat of his marksmanship. In the past this would have totally gone unnoticed and Korver would have received no credit for anything other than shots made, but the times, they are a'changin!

In tennis, video has long been used to analyze a player's strokes. And now, with computer analysis, a far more sophisticated analysis is possible. Unless a player has a major flaw, most of this work is done at the developmental level. For the most part, pros arrive, strokes intact, with strategy, tactics, conditioning and nerves the focus of their future development.

It's not uncommon for a player languishing in the mid-level rankings (40-100) to suddenly make a leap into the top 20 or higher. Something clicks and legitimate improvement occurs. David Ferrer is an excellent example. For years he was ranked in the mid 30s and then he started beating everyone below him and many above him and before you know it, Top Ten!

Modern analysis can't improve your conditioning, calm your nerves in tight situations, or give you the self-confidence to prevail in difficult situations, but it can bring insight into shot selection and patterns of play.

These supremely talented players believe they can make any shot in any situation. They can't. The best of them play within themselves, and like a great chess master or a giant python, exert pressure on their opponent until their will or their ribs crack.

There is no better example of this than the last metamorphosis of Andre Agassi. Agassi found his greatest success when he realized that pressuring his opponent by taking the ball early, something he was better at than anybody, and moving him side to side, he didn't need to hit the lines. He was taking time and angles and comfort from his opponent and sooner or later this would break him. Why flirt with the lines when deep, solid shots will get the job done?

In the U.S. Open final of 2010 rain and wind marred the first two sets of the final between Rafael Nadal and Novak Djokovic. After a rain delay, play resumed under near perfect conditions. Commentator John McEnroe correctly predicted that these two great players would put on a great show.

Into the fifth set they battled until Rafael Nadal finally prevailed in what was one of the most entertaining finals in U.S. Open history.

The match was decided by a few loose shots by Djokovic, especially a backhand down the line attempted winner from outside the alley. I don't believe this was lost on him. I remember specific shots from specific matches that took place years ago. I'm sure Djokovic does also.

In 2011 Novak Djokovic had one of the greatest years any male tennis player has ever had. Winning three of four Grand Slam tournaments, only losing a tough match to Nadal in the French, Novak was relentless in his pursuit of perfection. Gone were the loose shots and especially gone was that attempted backhand winner from off the court. Now, that situation produces a cross-court designed to keep him in the point until he has a down the line opportunity from within the court, rather than wide of it.

It's taken a long time to get to the point of this essay, which is: careful video analysis could point out the situations where a player consistently chooses the wrong shot and loses the point where other choices would have more favorable results. Maybe it's a shot from the wrong position, or with the wrong ball height, or the wrong situation, but these are the type of things that can be cleaned up and breakthroughs achieved. A 6-4 set has the winner winning 52% of the points. It doesn't take much to bring that back to 50-50.

I don't know if this is being done, but I know pros like Federer or Djokovic certainly have the resources to do this analysis and that the changes it would suggest would be a lot easier to incorporate into their games than a change to their forehand or serve. I know Djokovic became a better player after that 2010 loss to Nadal. Either through analysis or intuition those choices changed for Djokovic and you see the result. He is now the No. 1 player in the world. I don't know if this kind of video analysis helped, but I know that it could.

CHAPTER NINETEEN

They Said It

If you watch enough tennis, you begin to notice that almost no point goes uncommented on by at least one of the three(?) announcers in the booth. Over the course of five sets, and maybe as many hours, that's a lot of commenting. Some of these comments are insightful, even illuminating, stuff you can only get from a player who's been there and done that. I mean, I don't know what I'd be thinking in the fifth set on Center Court in a Grand Slam semi or final. I only know I'll never find out. The thoughts of McEnroe, Jim Courier or Chris Evert at times like these can genuinely add to my enjoyment of the match. Then there are the other times. The times where even though it's match point, I quickly hit the rewind button on my DVR because I can't believe he just said that. Alas, my ears are usually correct and the announcer did just say that. I only bring it up here, not to nitpick, but to explain to my readers that though these are fantastic athletes and skilled beyond belief tennis players, they do not possess the physics defying, godlike powers that Johnny Mac just gave them. No one does.

Here are three recent examples of these guys just losing their minds.

Pete Sampras vs Jim Courier in a seniors match with commentary by Jimmy Arias, another guy I generally respect. The point: Pete serves out wide from the deuce court and follows it to the net. Courier hits a relatively weak forehand down the line to Sampras's backhand volley. Courier runs to the open side only to have Sampras volley behind him for an easy point.

This serve and volley exchange is played out on hundreds of courts every day for ages. No magic here; at least no magic for you mere mortals. However, according to Mr. Arias, Pete moved in for the volley, and "held" the volley until Courier committed to cover the open court or stay where he was. Brilliant. Once he moved, Sampras hit the ball into the open court behind him.

I have a bit of a problem with this interpretation. Not even 14 time Grand Slam winner Pete Sampras can hold his volley for longer than the .003 to .008 seconds the ball usually stays on the strings, hardly long enough time to allow Courier to commit to anything. What really happens on these points is that Courier's weak return down the line forces him to scramble to the open court or to stay home. If he ain't scramblin' Pete will simply volley cross court for the winner. If he is, Pete will notice and volley behind him or not notice and still hit cross court where Courier will have a play on the ball. He can't wait for anything. He hits the ball when it's appropriate to hit the ball. Wait any longer and he'll probably miss the volley. Nothin' to see here folks. Just Tennis 101.

John McEnroe said something similar in the 2015 U.S. Open Final when Roger Federer took an easy backhand and hit it behind a flying Novak Djokovic. Federer did not wait on the shot. No one waits on the shot. He hit it when it was the right time to hit it. To do otherwise is to invite an error. Djokovic had long since departed and Federer had an easy winner.

Chris Evert was recently talking about Serena Williams' serve and why she was struggling. Chris explained that Serena was using her legs too early or too late (I forget which) and consequently wasn't throwing the ball high enough. This caused her to hit the ball on the way down rather than at the height of the toss.

Where to begin? If Serena's toss was too low it definitely could have caused her serving problems. Even though she wasn't a very natural server herself, Chris Evert should know that Serena, like most good servers, hit the ball on the way down, rather than at the height of the toss. Serena's perfect serve usually hits the ball after it drops a few inches, and not at the top. Players who do hit the ball at the top of the toss are usually described as "sneaky fast" or having a serve that "jumps on you quickly" because they are out of the norm. No one hits the ball on the way up. At least no one anyone has ever heard of. Roscoe Tanner, famous in the Borg-McEnroe era, was said to hit his excellent serve on the way up, but video analysis showed that even he hit it at the top or on the way down.

Novak Djokovic and Roger Federer recently competed in the year-end Tournament of Champions in London. Receiving in the Ad-court, Federer decided to move left to give himself a better chance to hit a big forehand on Djokovic's second serve. Unfortunately for Roger, Novak hit his second serve down the middle for an easy ace. The Tennis Channel announcers heaped praise on Djokovic for catching Roger's move out of "the corner of his eye" and changing the direction of his serve! Really? I think Jimmy Connors in a long ago match summed up the likelihood of this happening when he described a point this way. "I changed my mind midway through the shot and like every other time I changed my mind, I missed."
The other seven or eight times that Federer moved left to hit a forehand Djokovic hit the serve right where Roger hoped he would. He must not have seen him move "out of the corner of his eye" these times?

Finally, just to reiterate the earlier section on "anticipation", most remarkable plays in a quick exchange at the net or a stretch volley off a pass are not "anticipated" but a product of "see the ball, chase the ball." When a situation is more desperate, players often guess which way the ball is going. Sometimes they are right. Most often, they move early enough that the hitter can change the direction of the ball away from his opponent. Announcers always want to give the players more credit for their intuition and less to their amazing athleticism. I'm not sure why.

I only mention this because I have heard the average player lament the fact that they could not do what they had heard the pros do. They can't adjust, react, anticipate or read the shots as well as they think they should. The truth is that the pros don't do it very well either, but often the announcers tell you they can.

CHAPTER TWENTY

They Might Be Giants

John Isner, along with Kevin Anderson and especially Ivo Karlovic comprise the giants of the tennis world, at least the giants that regularly patrol the top 50 in the world. Blessed (?) with great height, their serves often make them unbreakable. I suppose if they were as nimble as the shrimpkins of the tennis world they would be signing max contracts for $50-100 million in the NBA, but they aren't. I find their footwork quite remarkable, but relatively speaking, the adjective most used to describe their movement is "lumbering."

This "lumbering" movement around the court during and especially after a point lends itself to a narrative that these giants are not particularly athletic and only reside in the top tier of tennis players because of their height. Nothing could be further from the truth.

In tennis, every so-called "advantage" has its' drawbacks. If you are short, you are generally quicker and perhaps more consistent as your groundstrokes have a smaller swing pattern. The angle for your serve is a little tougher and your reach at the net is a little less. If you are taller, your serving window is larger and your reach is greater. Longer arms mean a bigger swing pattern and with it the greater likelihood that things can be slightly amiss, which is all it takes to miss a shot. Those same long arms are a disadvantage for any balls aimed directly at you, and we have already touched on the quickness, or lack of, in those long legs.

Perhaps it is adapting to their large swing paths or adapting to still growing right up to maturity, but all three of these guys are playing the best tennis of their career as they approach 30, or as in Karlovic's case, 36. I discuss this at length in a later chapter (Magic, Jason and Fed), but the improvement is noticeable. Karlovic volleys and half-volleys like a man a foot shorter. Anderson made this year's quarterfinal in the U.S. Open with a decisive four set victory over Andy Murray and John Isner is on the verge of cracking the Top Ten.

I don't think they get enough credit for all this hard work. While many of their matches come down to tiebreakers, many are matches where they break serve but their opponent does not. When Djokovic does it, he's a great player. When Isner does it, he has a huge serve. It doesn't help that sweat starts dripping off Isner's cap in the first game or that Anderson and Karlovic walk around like storks between points.

Commentators look at these guys and almost always give the edge to their opponent because he "appears" fresher later in the match. No matter how many close, long matches these guys win, the perception lingers that they are more fatigued because they do not move around the court like David Ferrer or any of the other little Energizer bunnies out there.

In a recent match Isner's opponent was supposedly fresher and had the edge late in the match. Match point against Isner produced a 17 shot rally (longest of the match) with Isner's opponent missing a forehand from outside the alley. He never got another chance as Isner won the last four points.

I guess it's hard to relate to these guys because neither the commentators nor the rest of us can relate to the challenges faced by a 6'9" tennis player. That does not mean we can't appreciate their skills and give them their due. There are many, many 7' basketball players not good enough for the NBA, just as there are many very tall tennis players not in the ATP top 50.

Wilt Chamberlain, the only man to lead the NBA in rebounding and assists while only credited for being a big guy who could dunk, understood it first when he said "Nobody roots for Goliath."

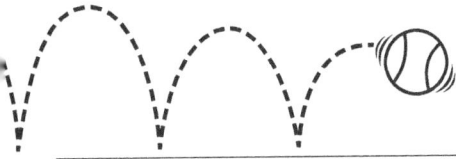

CHAPTER TWENTY ONE

Making America Great Again?

The United States, which once dominated the sport of tennis is currently struggling through one of the leaner periods in its history. With current standardbearers John Isner, Sam Querry and Jack Sock unable to crack the top ten and previous top Americans Andy Roddick and James Blake notching one U.S. Open victory between them, this millennium has been very tough on American men's tennis.

There are three common theories as to why this is, all, I guess, with some validity.

The first theory is that the USTA, which has lots of cash to throw at top juniors, either chooses badly or spoils those it does shower with money and opportunity. The argument is that the Europeans work harder, and perhaps it might be a little more egalitarian than the states in finding talent, where tennis is still a rich kid's sport.

The second argument is that Europeans grow up playing on clay and must learn how to construct points better, rather than letting a big serve or forehand make everything short and simple. This also plays into why the Spanish players are dominating. While this is true, I don't think it can still be relevant by the time a player turns pro. If you haven't learned how to construct a point emphasizing your strengths or exploiting your opponent's weaknesses by the time you are nineteen, it's unlikely you are ever going to learn that particular skill.

The last argument is that American athletes choose other sports over tennis. Baseball, basketball and football all offer far more money, and with the exception of basketball, far more opportunity than tennis. The Major Leagues employ over 700 players all making more than $500,000 a year with few expenses. Football employs even more with a similar minimum, and like baseball, very little foreign competition. The NBA is another story with very few players breaking into the league each season and also worldwide competition. Tennis, on the other hand is worldwide, doesn't pay nearly as well until you hit the top ten, and you have a ton of expenses as an individual out on tour.

All these arguments make some sense, but can't explain why Switzerland has two of the top five players in the world (Federer and Wawrinka) or why the Spanish players were dominating the sport for ten years but haven't produced any star replacement players or why Belgium, of all countries, recently had the number one and two female players (Henin and Clijsters) in the world. France always seems to have a large number of players in the top 100 but rarely in the top ten. Why?

I think truly great tennis players are where you find them. Federer and Wawrinka are Swiss, but Switzerland prior to these two only produced a handful of journeyman pros. I doubt that either one would credit the Swiss system exclusively for their success, or even their competition with one another.

Novak Djokovic was born to be number one and has let nothing get in his way in pursuit of that goal. Serbia has a solid tennis presence, but has not produced other champions.

Rafael Nadal is a freak of nature and while he no doubt benefited from the strong Spanish program, it's equally surprising that they didn't try to "fix" him.

Actually, Nadal isn't in the top five at the moment. That position is filled by Kei Nishikori from Japan who is the beneficiary of Project 44. Project 44 was the Japanese program to produce a top male player, specifically Nishikori. The program was named Project 44 because no Japanese male had ever been ranked higher than 44.

Andy Murray is from Scotland for God's sake. Scotland's last great player didn't even play in the last century. He played in the one before that. For the longest time Andy was coached by his Mom. Maybe this is the new formula for success.

In conclusion, if anyone had told you in 2000 that the top five players in the world would consist of a Serb, a Japanese, two Swiss and a Scot you would have thought he was nuts.

This U.S. lapse is probably temporary and will last until we have a star who captures the public imagination with a Grand Slam win. Americans seem to be uninterested in anything less.

When it does end, and Americans are winning again, the explanations for the new success will begin. Print and TV commentators will credit or blame the USTA, or the tennis academies or the new training methods. All will have some merit, none will be "The Answer!"

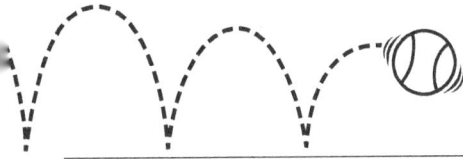

CHAPTER TWENTY TWO

I was wrong, and I'm Sorry

Like most married men, the title phrase is something I say every day, and multiple times on weekends, but rarely am I forced to say it about anything related to tennis. This weekend Roger Federer forced me to say it.

For many years now I have argued that Roger Federer, great as he is, is not as great as those 17 Grand Slam titles would indicate, and I had a very logical argument why that was the case.

First and foremost was the fact that Roger acquired a great many of those titles in a vacuum, not in the top heavy talent pool that he is playing in now. From 2003 at Wimbledon to the U.S. Open in 2008 Roger won 12 of the 18 Grand Slam events played, but going 2-4 against Nadal in finals. Without Nadal, Roger might have won 16 of 18 events. This is remarkable consistency, but against whom? With the exception of an aged and injured Andre Agassi, there are not a lot of hall of famers amongst the vanquished.

Secondly is his dismal record against Rafael Nadal. My argument was that when a formidable opponent does appear, Roger is not equal to the task. He loses decisively on clay, wins a couple of times on grass, his best surface, but Nadal beats him there as well. Nadal leads 23-10 overall, 14-6 in finals, 9-2 in grand Slams, 6-2 in Grand Slam finals.

Finally, when Novak Djokovic and Andy Murray achieve Grand Slam Championship status, 2011, Federer is only able to sneak one more title in, U.S. Open 2012.

Both Djokovic and Nadal are superior to Roger, Rafa from 2008-2011, and Novak since.

There's my case against Roger Federer as the greatest of all time. In fact, I have been known to say over and over again that the best tennis ever played is a good Nadal versus Djokovic match.

That was until yesterday, Sunday August 23rd, 2015. It was then that I saw Federer overwhelm Novak Djokovic only one day after destroying Andy Murray. Yes it was Cincinnatti where Federer has now won the title seven times. And yes, Djokovic and Murray had come off a long week in Montreal playing both singles and doubles and had played more this week as well.

It doesn't matter. Atop the ATP leader board for breaking serve are Djokovic and Murray at around 33%. Total service breaks combined against Federer – 0! In fact, Federer didn't lose his serve the entire tournament. When Feliciano Lopez played three marvelous points in the quarterfinals to get to 0-40, Federer came up with three magnificent serves and that was all she wrote. Murray was totally overwhelmed and while Djokovic lost the first set in a tiebreak, the relentless pressure Roger was putting on his serve while holding quite easily himself made a Federer victory inevitable, no matter how the tiebreak fared.

Roger has always been a great server, but now, several years past 30, I think he is even better. His ability to consistently serve to his spots with great speed and spin has never been better. And when I say consistently, I don't mean 60% or 70%. I mean that each and every service game is won with multiple good first serves. He doesn't have bad service games, no matter what the overall statistics might say. It's not enough to have a high percentage of winning serves if once or twice a set you have none. Roger does not do that.

His groundstrokes have never been better as he takes the ball earlier and puts more pressure on his opponent. His movement looks as good as ever. Has he lost half a step? I can't detect it. And now his commitment to the attacking game is complete after being ambivalent the last several years.

All this forces me to rethink my opinion of him as the greatest ever.

Yes, he played in a weak era from 2003 – 2007, but he took full advantage. His consistency in reaching Grand Slam finals in those years has never been close to being duplicated. From 2005 Wimbledon to 2008 U.S. Open Roger made all 10 finals, winning all but two French Opens to Nadal.

Yes, he has a losing record to Nadal, but I am forced to concede that Raphael Nadal is a freak of nature. I say that not because of his incredible dominance on clay or his overall record but because his incredibly successful style has not been imitated in all these years. No one hits their forehand like Rafa, at least no one who has made the tour. Gregor Dimitrov storms onto the tennis scene in 2009 and earns the nickname "Baby Fed." There are no "Baby Rafas." Rafa's style was perfectly suited to defeat Roger and accounts for at least some of his success against him. Roger's average height and one-handed backhand are no match for the very heavy topspin and high, explosive bounce of Nadal's forehand. Taller players with two handed backhands and lesser rankings were often able to beat Nadal when Roger couldn't.

Lastly, Djokovic and Murray have had success against Roger, but not overwhelmingly and they are in their prime and Roger a bit past his. And let's not forget that Roger Federer is still dominating everyone else. Yes, occasionally he does not bring his "A" game, but that's to be expected at 34. I remember watching aging stars like Chris Evert and Jimmy Connors just totally unable to produce their best tennis on certain days. But those days are still rare. At 34 he is a little more vulnerable in a fifth set, but he was never great in those anyway.

In conclusion, I have to admit that Roger Federer has a legitimate claim to being the best of all time, at least more legitimate that I've given him in the past.

I was wrong, and I'm sorry.

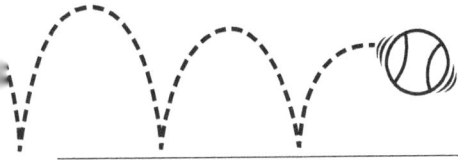

CHAPTER TWENTY THREE

Tucker

Tucker Callahan is a player. He walks like a player. He carries himself like a player. He is among the best of his generation.

Tucker Callahan is four years old. He can rally with foam balls, low compression balls, regular balls and I suspect, if he had to, baseballs.

He's no newcomer. He's been dragging people to hit with him since he was 2 ½. He has a full, smooth service motion. He is equally at home on a short court, 60' court or a full-sized court. He can slice and hit topspin. His backhand is two handed, but he is quickly learning a one-handed slice. He volleys like a seven year old!

When he plays points with talented, but mortal kids I swear he gives them points just to keep them trying. I don't know how he knows to do this, he just knows. It's freaky.

Tucker's seven year old sister Savannah plays tennis, but has already decided to not give it her full concentration, at least partly because she knows she can't compete with her little brother.

So what does the future hold for Tucker? I'm confident he'll be the best 5, 6, 7 and 8 year old in the area, whatever area he lives in. It takes quite a while to catch up to someone so precocious. Beyond that? I don't know.

His mother was an outstanding Division I College player who remains active in coaching the sport, so the genetics are there as well as the access to coaching and facilities.

Anything is possible, but anyone who thinks they know what the future holds for Tucker is kidding themselves. So many things have to fall into place for someone to make it to the pros. Temperament, dedication, physical gifts and luck all have to be there to succeed. So many things can sidetrack the dream. Distractions come in all shapes and sizes and injury can always be hiding just around the corner.

I don't where Tucker's tennis career will peak, but of these two things I am sure.

If Tucker makes it to the Pros, the Nick Bolletieri of his generation will be there to say on national television "From the first time I saw him, I knew he was going to be a champion." In all fairness, this may be true. What goes unmentioned is the same prediction for the dozens of kids who were similarly precocious and who never made it. Saying that, however, might tarnish his guru status.

Let's just imply that you saw qualities in him that you didn't see in the others and leave it at that.

Before you think I'm trashing the latest well-known teaching savant exclusively, let me assure you there is plenty of room for the locals. If Tucker does make it to tennis prominence just about every local pro worth his ego will be more than happy to tell you how he helped Tucker at an important stage of his development.

For the record, that important stage will have been whenever their paths crossed. Everyone loves a winner!

I don't know what Tucker's tennis future looks like or if he even has one. For now, I just love to watch someone do so effortlessly what so many of the rest of us struggle to do even marginally, and to do it oblivious to the fact that he is so special. I guess that's one of the special things about being four years old.

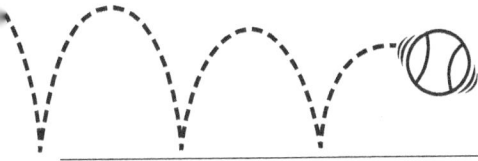

CHAPTER TWENTY FOUR

Observations: Immigrants

It's hard to go to a high level junior tournament in the U.S. and stand among the parents and not hear English with a foreign accent. I'm not talking about international events, just your run-of-the-mill regional junior event. As I said in my sections touching on junior tennis, it takes a certain type of parent to get a child to the top levels of tennis and apparently immigrants are often those parents.

I'm not sure how right-wing, anti-immigrant Republicans would react to this since they don't make many appearances at these events. "**They** are taking away American tennis jobs" doesn't have the right ring to it. "**They** are forcing down tennis wages" isn't right either. How can I make this piece anti-immigrant?

People new to this country often do find it to be "The Land of Opportunity" and attempt to take full advantage of that opportunity. Some become quite successful but many work to make their children even more successful. For those with resources, tennis success is attainable through patience, hard work, dedication and training. The time and expense this requires is something immigrant parents are willing to expend, more so than the average American parent.

Before you make that last statement into a pro or anti-immigrant sentence, remember that I have stated that Pro tennis players themselves often don't think this is the right path for their families.

Remember, this is just an observation. I leave you to interpret it as you will.

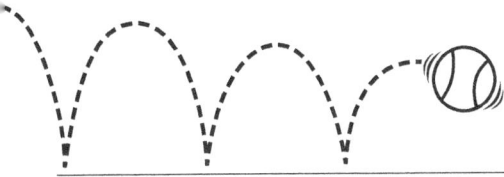

Epilogue

"There are a thousand thoughts lying within a man that he does not know till he takes up a pen to write."

WILLIAM MAKEPEACE THACKERAY

I hope you have enjoyed the thoughts expressed herein. If my slant on these tennis topics was entertaining or made you think about these things differently, I accomplished my goal.

Any comments, positive or negative, will be gladly considered at: davetennisdave@msn.com. I would love to know if I'd had any effect on any of my readers.

I have found the above quote to be very true, at least in my case. There are at least a thousand ideas in my head, all competing for the chance to be let out on paper. And no, it's not just tennis ideas. It's all kind of ideas. Politics for sure. Quirky human nature? It's in there. Comments on relationships? Oh, I've got 'em. All trying to get out. All hoping to be read by people like you. I don't know where to start and I definitely don't know how to stop. Make me stop!

Years from now, people will say "All the clues were there." No one paid any attention, or if they did, they thought someone else would take care of the problem. Someone else would read and realize and react before another book came out, but if you don't, no one will.

You know I can self-publish. No gatekeeper. The marketplace of ideas is an open air market now. There is nothing to stop me, only you, the discerning reader, can keep me from thinking that I write like the angels.

The next book is on you. Sure, after that, others will be as complicit as you, but the damage will have already been done. I'll believe that I can write, and write I will, and there's no telling where that will lead.

You have been warned.

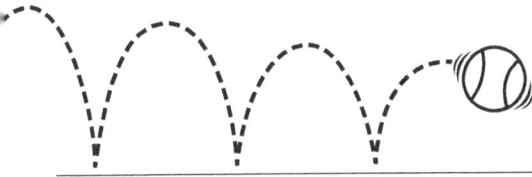

Acknowledgements

I would like to thank Bill Dowdall, Bev Kirby, Lauren Betz, Suzanne Farrell, Audrey Cohn and Jeff Jones for their help and encouragement. I'd also like to thank Mike Gelen for the cover and Joe Galanti for the layout.

A special shout out to all the strangers who gave my first book such positive reviews.

www.ingramcontent.com/pod-product-compliance
Lightning Source LLC
Chambersburg PA
CBHW070645030426
42337CB00020B/4178